STUDY GUIDE

The Lord's Prayer

R. Albert Mohler Jr.

LIGONIER MINISTRIES

Renew your Mind.

LIGONIER.ORG | 800-435-4343

1

Teach Us to Pray

INTRODUCTION

Who better to teach us how to pray than the Lord Jesus Christ? The disciples understood this, and as followers of Jesus Christ, we understand this. In this lesson, Dr. Mohler places the Lord's Prayer in the context of the Gospels.

LESSON OBJECTIVES

1. To answer why it is that we need to be taught how to pray
2. To introduce the context of the Lord's Prayer in Matthew and Luke

SCRIPTURE READING

Lord, teach us to pray, as John taught his disciples.

—Luke 11:1b

LECTURE OUTLINE

A. Christians need to be taught how to pray in order to guard against any confusion surrounding prayer and understand how prayer reveals what we actually believe.

1. Jesus taught His disciples to pray, and the record of His instruction can be found in two gospels, Matthew and Luke.

2. Like Jesus' disciples, we need to be taught how to pray because of the confusion that exists concerning prayer.
   a. Prayer can often fail to resemble the models of prayer found in the New Testament.
   b. Prayer can often be used to merely transition from one activity to the next even in the course of Christian worship.

3. Like Jesus' disciples, we need to be taught how to pray because prayer reveals what we actually believe.

       a.   Roger Scruton is a contemporary and prominent philosopher who converted to Christianity from atheism.

       b.   Even as an unbeliever, he rightly observed that a systematic theology reveals far less about what we believe than prayer.

       c.   Prayer not only reveals what we believe about God, it also reveals the entire range of our theological beliefs.

   4. The Lord's Prayer is the model by which Jesus taught us how to pray in order to guard against confusion so that we would pray what we believe.

       a.   The Lord's Prayer is short but theologically massive, because it includes the totality of the Christian faith.

       b.   The Lord's Prayer is the title traditionally given for the model Jesus gave the disciples.

B. The Lord's Prayer can be found in the gospel of Matthew and the gospel of Luke.

   1. The Lord's Prayer is found in Matthew 6 and Luke 11, which provide context important for understanding the Lord's Prayer.

       a.   Matthew 6 contains the form of the Lord's Prayer that has been used most often in the church and situates the prayer at the climactic peak of the Sermon on the Mount.

       b.   Luke 11 contains a shorter version of the Lord's Prayer but provides the greater context in which Jesus taught His disciples how to pray.

       c.   The context that Luke 11 provides helps us to understand why we have multiple accounts.

   2. The context of Jesus' instruction of the disciples in Luke 11 teaches us about Jesus' prayer life and teaching methodology.

       a.   Jesus habitually withdrew in order to pray; He would withdraw even from fellowship with the disciples into fellowship with the Father.

       b.   Luke 11:1 teaches us that Jesus was being observed in prayer, perhaps sovereignly anticipating His disciples' request.

       c.   Jesus is purposeful in allowing His disciples' request; question and answer can be a powerful and dynamic method of instruction.

       d.   Luke 11 teaches us that the nature of discipleship is being taught, so we must understand our need of being taught how to pray and honor the model of prayer Jesus gave to us.

C. The gospel of Matthew provides further context to the Lord's Prayer in sequence with Jesus' wider teaching on prayer—most particularly, how not to pray.

   1. Jesus teaches us not to pray hypocritically.

       a.   Jesus identifies the Pharisees as hypocrites, because they "love to stand and pray . . . that they may be praised by others" (Matt. 6:5).

       b.   Hypocrisy is presenting oneself as something one is not or presenting oneself one way in a given context while presenting oneself in another way in another context.

c. Jesus is teaching His disciples that the temptation to draw attention to ourselves is a persistent temptation in prayer.

2. Jesus teaches us not to pray ritualistic, empty prayers.

a. Jesus identifies the Gentiles as those that "heap up empty phrases . . . that they will be heard for their many words" (Matt. 6:7).

b. Prayer that is characteristically repetitious and ritualistic or prayer that is often accompanied by a symbolic object is not true prayer.

c. Repeated phrases and words may be appropriate in the context of urgency but do not fit the context of everyday Christian devotion.

d. Martin Luther said that Christian prayer should be "short and profound."

D. The Lord's Prayer has been honored throughout the history of the Christian church, because God's people have always understood their need to be taught how to pray.

1. The disciples needed to be taught how to pray, so we shouldn't be ashamed to acknowledge that we also need to be taught how to pray.

2. Christians throughout the centuries return again and again to the Lord's Prayer because it is how Jesus taught us to pray.

3. We often pray beyond the words of the Lord's Prayer, but we will never pray beyond the theology of the Lord's Prayer if we are faithful.

STUDY QUESTIONS

1. The Lord's Prayer is found in each of the Synoptic Gospels.
   a. True
   b. False

2. Jesus warns against _____ prayer.
   a. Ritualistic
   b. Repetitious
   c. Hypocritical
   d. All of the above

3. Jesus points out the hypocrisy of the prayers of the _____ .
   a. Zealots
   b. Essenes
   c. Pharisees
   d. Sadducees

4. The Lord's Prayer is the traditional title for the model prayer that Jesus gave His disciples, but other prayers can appropriately be called "The Lord's Prayer."
   a. True
   b. False

5. The disciple who asked Jesus to teach them how to pray was _____ .
    a. Peter
    b. Andrew
    c. Matthew
    d. Not identified

6. _____ said that Christian prayer should be "short and profound."
    a. Calvin
    b. Luther
    c. Spurgeon
    d. Augustine

DISCUSSION QUESTIONS

1. How do the gospel of Matthew and the gospel of Luke complement each other by providing the context of the Lord's Prayer? What do multiple gospel accounts teach us about the wisdom of God and Scripture?

2. Jesus gave us a model of how we are to pray. How is it possible that we are able to go beyond the words of the Lord's Prayer and remain faithful to the way Jesus taught us to pray?

3. What are some practical ways for Christians to avoid hypocritical and empty prayers?

4. How do discipleship and prayer relate to one another? What does the disciples' need to be taught how to pray teach us about ourselves?

2

Two Models of Prayer

INTRODUCTION

Not only did Jesus teach us how to pray, He taught us how not to pray. In this lesson, Dr. Mohler uses the parable of the Pharisee and the tax collector and common misconceptions about prayer to further introduce the Lord's Prayer.

LESSON OBJECTIVES

1. To contrast the prayers in the parable of the Pharisee and tax collector
2. To discuss the pervasive misconceptions about the nature of prayer

SCRIPTURE READING

But the tax collector, standing far off, would not even lift up his eyes to heaven, but beat his breast, saying, "God, be merciful to me, a sinner!" I tell you, this man went down to his house justified, rather than the other.

—Luke 18:13–14a

LECTURE OUTLINE

A. Jesus gave us the Lord's Prayer to teach us how to pray, but He also gave us other models of prayer that teach us how not to pray.

1. The parable of the Pharisee and the tax collector is primarily about the doctrine of justification, but it also teaches us something about prayer.
   a. The parable of the Pharisee and tax collector contains two models of prayer—one proper and one improper.
   b. Jesus told this parable to "some who trusted in themselves that they were righteous, and treated others with contempt" (Luke 18:9).
2. The parable of the Pharisee and the tax collector would have been perceived as theologically revolutionary because the tax collector went home justified.

a. Tax collectors were despised, known for their financial misdeeds against their own people in collusion with the Roman Empire.

b. Pharisees are notorious because of the New Testament witness, but they attempted to prove their obedience by exceeding the Mosaic law.

c. Pharisees were nonetheless guilty of legalism in their selectivity and failure to acknowledge their inability to fulfill the law's demands.

B. Jesus contrasted the prayers of the Pharisee and the tax collector to teach us about the justification and how much prayer reveals our theological understanding of it.

1. Jesus taught His disciples against the backdrop of the false teachings about prayer that are prominently demonstrated in the prayer of the Pharisee.

a. The Pharisee prayed standing by himself with horizontal concerns, trapped in a legalistic framework that required him to justify himself.

b. Like the Pharisee, if our prayers begin with reference to ourselves or to others, we are not praying as Jesus taught us how to pray.

c. The Pharisee's prayer is a hypocritical comparison of himself to other sinners and contains no confession of sin.

d. The Pharisee is self-deceived and, in effect, is attempting to deceive God by boasting of his spiritual devotion, his self-righteousness.

2. Jesus contrasted the prayer of the Pharisee with the prayer of the tax collector, "God, be merciful to me, a sinner!" (Luke 18:13).

a. The tax collector's prayer is very short, but it is a model of how an entire theological system can be concisely revealed in a few words.

b. Martin Luther's dying words are another example: *"Wir sind Bettler. Hoc est verum,"* translated, "We are beggars. This is true."

c. Standing, like the Pharisee, but far off, unlike the Pharisee, the tax collector is not drawing attention to himself.

d. The tax collector would not lift up his eyes toward heaven, which teaches us why bowing our heads in prayer is a Christian tradition.

e. Bowing our heads in prayer is a biblical picture that while not required often directs our hearts Godward in humble confession.

C. The context of the Lord's Prayer in Matthew 6 teaches us that prayer is a normative and natural part of the Christian life.

1. Prayer is a normative part of the Christian life.

a. Jesus taught His disciples how to pray in the context of the refrain "when you pray" and not "if you pray."

b. Christ expects His people to be constant in prayer.

2. Prayer is a natural part of the Christian life.

a. Prayer is possible because we are made in the image of God, which means we can know, relate, worship, and obey Him.

b. All of creation reflects the glory of God, but only we can consciously declare the glory of God.

    c. From the beginning, God intended to be in conversation with us, and in a fallen world, prayer is the only way to carry on that conversation.

D. Knowing how not to pray helps us understand how to pray.
1. Prayer is not creative self-expression.
    a. Prayer is not an opportunity to be creative, but it is an opportunity to be expressive.
    b. Praying the Scripture is truly expressive, helping us to find the words to pray and reminding us that God speaks through Scripture.
2. Prayer is not therapy.
    a. Studies conducted on the therapeutic effects of prayer can tempt us into the cultural trap of believing that mere prayer is good for us.
    b. Prayer is good for us, but prayer is not merely therapeutic, because it has theological content.
3. Prayer is not manipulation.
    a. A temptation in prayer is to use manipulative language when we know people are overhearing us.
    b. Prayer can also be used manipulatively toward God and ourselves in an attempt to elicit a spiritual sensation to gauge our spiritual health.
4. Prayer is not negotiation.
    a. Negotiation may be a natural part of our everyday lives, but we cannot address ourselves to God as if we are negotiation with Him.
    b. Even in Abraham's intercession for the cities of the valley, God was making a point to Abraham (Gen. 18:22–33; 19:29).
5. Prayer is not informing God of what He doesn't know.
    a. The fact that God knows what we need before we even ask may tempt us to ask, "Why pray?"
    b. The mystery of prayer is that God has sovereignly willed that His people will ask Him for what they need.

STUDY QUESTIONS

1. The main point of the parable of the Pharisee and the tax collector is the disposition of our heart in prayer.
    a. True
    b. False

2. The form of Judaism practiced during the earthly ministry of Jesus Christ is called _____ Temple Judaism.
    a. Old
    b. New
    c. First
    d. Second

3. Martin Luther called us _____ in need of mercy in his dying words, *"Wir sind Bettler. Hoc est verum."*
   a. Sinners
   b. Beggars
   c. Pharisees
   d. Publicans

4. Jesus highlighted the Pharisee's standing posture in prayer as evidence of the Pharisee's hypocrisy.
   a. True
   b. False

5. Prayer as an act of _____ is not true prayer.
   a. Adoration
   b. Confession
   c. Persuasion
   d. Thanksgiving

6. Prayer used only to stimulate religious feelings is prayer as an act of _____ .
   a. Negotiation
   b. Manipulation
   c. Harmonization
   d. Self-expression

DISCUSSION QUESTIONS

1. What is significant about the posture of the Pharisee and the tax collector in prayer? How has this helped you to understand traditions surrounding prayer throughout church history?

2. Prayer reveals our theology. What does the content of the prayers of the Pharisee and the tax collector reveal about their theology? Who is more orthodox? Why?

3. Dr. Mohler identified some common misconceptions about prayer. Are you susceptible to any of these misconceptions? Which do you consider the most dangerous? Why?

4. How does our understanding of ourselves and our understanding of God shape the way we pray?

3

Our Father

INTRODUCTION

The Lord's Prayer opens with the words "Our Father," an amazing declaration of our relationship to God through Jesus Christ. In this lesson, Dr. Mohler explores the wonder of how it is that Christians are able to pray to God as Father.

LESSON OBJECTIVES

1. To uncover the unity provided to us by the Lord's Prayer
2. To underscore the doctrine of adoption in the Lord's Prayer
3. To confront modern distortions of the Fatherhood of God

SCRIPTURE READING

Holy Father, keep them in your name, which you have given me, that they may be one, even as we are one.

—John 17:11b

But you have received the Spirit of adoption as sons, by whom we cry, "Abba! Father!"

—Romans 8:15b

And because you are sons, God has sent the Spirit of his Son into our hearts, crying, "Abba! Father!"

—Galatians 4:6

LECTURE OUTLINE

A. The Lord's Prayer has united Christians throughout the centuries.

1. The Lord's Prayer reveals the gift of God's revelation in Scripture; when Jesus taught His disciples how to pray, He taught us how to pray.

2. The Lord's Prayer militates against the modern tendency toward individualism, because the first person plural pronoun is used throughout the prayer.

3. In praying the Lord's Prayer, we are united in the truth, as Jesus prayed we would be in the High Priestly Prayer (John 17).
    a. Historically, ecumenism reduces Christianity to the lowest common denominator to create a facade of Christian unity.
    b. Jesus prayed for the unity of His disciples to be based on the truth of God's Word, so true Christian unity is a theologically based unity.
    c. In the Lord's Prayer, Jesus teaches us to pray a robustly theological prayer so that even our prayers will demonstrate Christian unity.

4. One of the great gifts God has given to His church is a unity in prayer.
    a. The Lord's Prayer defies how language changes over time, such that the same prayer that the Apostles prayed is the same prayer we pray.
    b. The first-person-plural pronoun of the Lord's Prayer suggests that we are never alone, that we are united with every generation, in the faith.

B. Christians are able to pray to God as Father because we have been adopted.

1. Jesus taught us to pray to God as Father—a single-word theological revolution.
    a. In the Old Testament, God is referred to as "Father" fourteen times and only in reference to being the Father of Israel corporately.
    b. The Israelites knew God as the Father of Israel but did not pray to Him intimately as Father.

2. We are able to pray to God as Father based on the authority of Jesus Christ and the atonement of Jesus Christ.
    a. Jesus Christ taught us to pray as the incarnate Son of God, the only One who had the eternal right to refer to the Father as His Father.
    b. Jesus Christ secured for us the knowledge of God as Father through the atonement—we have been adopted as sons and daughters.

3. The doctrine of the adoption is one of the most powerful teachings about our salvation in the New Testament (Rom. 8:14–17; Gal. 4:4–5; Eph. 1:5).
    a. Jesus Christ accomplished the adoption of those who would become His brothers and sisters—His joint heirs—through the atonement.
    b. We are able to pray to God as Father because the Spirit bears witness to what God has done for us in Christ.
    c. We no longer pray to God as a corporate Father of Israel; we pray to God as Father because the Father has adopted us in Christ.

C. Protestant liberalism and ideological feminism have challenged orthodox definitions of the Fatherhood of God.

1. Protestant liberalism attempted to redefine Christianity in the nineteenth and twentieth centuries.
    a. Protestant liberalism rationalized the supernatural out of Christianity.
    b. Protestant liberalism in the form of unitarianism denied the deity of Jesus Christ and, in turn, undercut substitutionary atonement.

        c. Gospel-less Christianity—a Christianity without biblical authority—leads to mere spiritual moralism.

  2. Protestant liberalism attempted to redefine the Fatherhood of God.

        a. Protestant liberalism's questioning of the atonement meant that the Fatherhood of God had to be redefined.

        b. The Fatherhood of God only makes sense in light of the atoning work of Jesus Christ, the work that makes our adoption possible.

  3. Protestant liberalism failed to make a distinction between the Fatherhood of God over creation and the Fatherhood of God over those in Christ.

        a. God's fatherly care is on display in creation, and He is sovereign over all of creation, so in that sense He is a Father to all His creation.

        b. God is Father over all of creation, but only those who have been adopted by Him through Christ can pray to Him as "Our Father."

  4. Feminist theology and the rise of ideological feminism created challenges to the Fatherhood of God.

        a. The spread of feminism in liberal Protestant denominations lead to inclusive language proposals for God to be addressed as "Mother."

        b. The presuppositions of gender inclusivity lead to the insistence that any reference to God as "Father" was an inadequate metaphor.

D. All language is analogical, yet God has revealed Himself to us analogically.

  1. All language is analogical, so our language about God is analogical, but that does not mean that our understanding of God as Father is metaphorical.

        a. Metaphor is a category of analogical speech by which we are able to compare or contrast one thing to another.

        b. The Bible doesn't compare God to a father, saying that God is *like* our father; the Bible says God *is* our Father.

  2. Scripture is inerrant and infallible, so we must honor it as such, distinguishing when it uses metaphorical and clearly analogical language.

STUDY QUESTIONS

1. Historically, ecumenism is known for successfully producing theologically based unity.

    a. True

    b. False

2. God is only referred to as "Father" _____ times in the Old Testament.

    a. Two

    b. Seven

    c. Twelve

    d. Fourteen

3. The doctrine of _____ helps to clarify how it is that Christians are even able to pray the Lord's Prayer.
   a. Creation
   b. Adoption
   c. Glorification
   d. Sanctification

4. The Bible never speaks metaphorically about God as our Father.
   a. True
   b. False

5. Ideological feminism proposed _____ language that questioned the Father-hood of God.
   a. Neutral
   b. Evolving
   c. Inclusive
   d. Progressive

6. We speak _____ , but God speaks _____ .
   a. Analogically; ontologically
   b. Analogically; metaphorically
   c. Metaphorically; analogically
   d. Metaphorically; ontologically

DISCUSSION QUESTIONS

1. How is Christian unity demonstrated in the Lord's Prayer? In what ways can meditating on your unity with Christ and your unity with fellow believers change the way you pray?

2. How significant and in what way does the person and work of Christ change the way we relate and pray to God? How does unitarianism threaten the foundational truths upon which we pray?

3. How did Protestant liberalism attempt to redefine the Fatherhood of God? How is this at odds with biblical Christianity?

4. How does the challenge of ideological feminism to the Fatherhood of God relate to language? How would you counter these contemporary claims?

4

A Holy Name

INTRODUCTION

The Lord's Prayer reveals to us that the Father to whom we pray is holy and transcendent. In this lesson, Dr. Mohler explains the important distinctions that need to be made to understand the holiness of God.

LESSON OBJECTIVES

1. To describe God's transcendence and God's holiness
2. To clarify what it means to pray, "Hallowed be your name"

SCRIPTURE READING

Ascribe to the Lord the glory due his name; bring an offering and come before him! Worship the Lord in the splendor of holiness; tremble before him all the earth.

—1 Chronicles 16:29–30a

LECTURE OUTLINE

A. When we pray, "Our Father in heaven," we are speaking of the God of the Bible—the one true, living, and eternal God who is transcendent in His glory.

1. The Bible describes the transcendence of God in terms of heaven as the realm of God's existence.

2. We are limited in our own capacity to fully comprehend a transcendent and infinite God, but God has revealed Himself to us in Scripture.

   a. The Old Testament prohibitions on idolatry created a sharp contrast between God as revealed to Israel and the surrounding paganism.

   b. God is revealed as dwelling in heaven, and just as Paul proclaimed in Athens, He "does not live in temples made by man" (Acts 17:24).

3. The distinction between Creator and creation is central to Christian theology.

     a. The theology of the Bible—Christian theology—reveals that God is transcendent above the earth that He created (Deut. 4:39, 33:26).

     b. People will only know that we pray to God Most High if we do not blur the lines between Creator and creation (Ps. 97:9).

  4. The opening phrases of the Lord's Prayer reveal to us the transcendence of God and our yearning for Him as Father.

     a. Psychologists and psychiatrists identify fatherlessness as a modern-day epidemic.

     b. One of the great promises of the gospel is that even the fatherless have a Father in God through Jesus Christ.

B. The first petition of the Lord's Prayer, "Hallowed be your name," continues to point us to the fullness of God's perfections and our experience of them.

  1. "Hallowed" is present in modern English translations of the Bible.

     a. In many modern-English translations, "art" is replaced by "is" and "thy" is replaced by "your," but "hallowed" remains.

     b. We do not have a word in our modern vocabulary that conveys the meaning of "hallowed" in such a way that it could be replaced.

  2. "Hallowed" immediately raises the question of how it is that God's name could be made more holy.

     a. God is infinite in all His perfections, and we cannot add or take away from His attributes.

     b. In order to make sense of what is meant when we pray, "Hallowed be your name," distinctions have to be made.

  3. The Bible speaks in two different dimensions, so when we speak of glorifying God, we are speaking reasonably.

     a. The Bible speaks of a glory that is God's glory, infinite and eternal.

     b. The Bible also speaks of a glory that is God's glory, but that is the visible manifestation of His glory in creation.

     c. When we speak of glorifying God, we are speaking about our desire to see God's glory displayed more visibly on earth.

  4. God's holiness is in the same category as God's glory.

     a. When we pray, "Hallowed be your name," we are praying that God's holiness would be demonstrated and increasingly recognized.

     b. God is hallowing His name in creation through us as we engage the culture and declare the gospel until Christ returns.

C. All of Scripture testifies to the holiness of God, but the call of the prophet Isaiah in particular helps us to understand what it means for God to be defined as holy.

  1. The famous passage on the holiness of God is the call of Isaiah.

     a. In Isaiah 6, the prophet sees a vision of God enthroned high and lifted up, with His glory filling the temple.

     b. He saw seraphim that called to each other saying, "Holy, holy, holy is the LORD of hosts; the whole earth is full of his glory" (Isa. 6:3).

2. "Holy, holy, holy" is the highest expression of the holiness of God.
   a. The threefold repetition, "Holy, holy, holy," is called the Trisagion.
   b. Hebrew does not have comparatives or superlatives, so the only way to stress the extent of God's holiness is to repeat it three times.
3. Isaiah could not avert his eyes from his vision of God and was faced with his own sinfulness.
   a. Like Isaiah, we are simultaneously attracted and repulsed by the holiness of God.
   b. We are attracted because we are made in the image of God, but we are repulsed because we are sinful creatures.
   c. The response of sinful creatures to the holiness of God is hatred because God's holiness further exposes our sinfulness.

D. The first petition of the Lord's Prayer is in particular reference to God's name.
   1. God attaches special significance to His name throughout the Bible
      a. He revealed Himself to Moses as "I am who I am" (Ex. 3:14), and revealed Himself to Pharaoh and the Egyptians as the Lord in power.
      b. In the Lord's Prayer, Jesus reveals to us that we are to pray to God by His name as our Father that His name would be hallowed.
   2. God loves His name—it discloses Himself and is His personal possession.
      a. As His creatures, we are to hallow His name.
      b. We need to be very careful to only use His name as He would have us to use it: obedient to Him, never in vain.

STUDY QUESTIONS

1. The opening address of the Lord's Prayer, "Our Father in heaven," should prompt us to reflect on God's immanence.
   a. True
   b. False

2. Paul confronted the idolatry of _____ by declaring that God "does not live in temples made by man."
   a. Rome
   b. Athens
   c. Ephesus
   d. Macedonia

3. God's threefold holiness, "Holy, holy, holy," is particularly announced in the books of _____.
   a. Psalms and Isaiah
   b. Hebrews and Revelation
   c. Psalms and Proverbs
   d. Isaiah and Revelation

4. The Creator-creature distinction is a hallmark of pagan prayer.
   a. True
   b. False

5. The threefold repetition of the seraphim crying out, "Holy, holy, holy," is called the _____ .
   a. Triplex
   b. Trivium
   c. Tribrach
   d. Trisagion

6. Dr. Mohler mentioned that the furtherance of the _____ mandate would work to display God's holiness in the theater of creation.
   a. Ethical
   b. Biblical
   c. Cultural
   d. Social

DISCUSSION QUESTIONS

1. What do you think are the essential elements to prayer that would communicate to others that you are praying to the one true God?

2. What distinctions should we make about God's holiness when considering the first petition of the Lord's Prayer, "Hallowed be your name"?

3. How do you resolve the seeming contradiction that we are simultaneously attracted to and repulsed by the holiness of God? How is this pictured for us in Isaiah's vision?

4. When you pray, "Hallowed by your name," in what ways are you hoping to see God answer your prayer in the world, especially using you as a means?

5

City of God

INTRODUCTION

When we pray the Lord's Prayer, we pray for Christ's right-now rule and reign to be extended over all the earth. In this lesson, Dr. Mohler explains how Christians are to live and to pray as dual citizens until Christ's kingdom is fully realized.

LESSON OBJECTIVES

1. To contrast theologically rich prayer with theologically empty prayer
2. To outline a strategy for us to know how to live in the "already but not yet"

SCRIPTURE READING

The kingdom of heaven is at hand.

—Matthew 10:7b

The kingdom of the world has become the kingdom of our Lord and his Christ, and he shall reign forever and ever.

—Revelation 11:15b

LECTURE OUTLINE

A. Scripture teaches us the importance of prayer, especially as it concerns God's name.
   1. The third commandment points to the care we must use with God's name.
      a. Our language can rob God of His glory, and some language is even intended to rob God of His glory.
      b. Every idle word we ever speak will be judged, so we must be especially careful how we use God's name.
   2. The first petition of the Lord's Prayer clarifies the fact that we cannot fulfill God's command by simply avoiding certain words.

     a. When we pray, "Hallowed be your name," we are praying that God's glory will be made manifest, visible, and clear.

     b. The Lord's Prayer requires that we actively pursue what it means to demonstrate the power and integrity of God's name.

  3. We need to fear and stand in awe of God's name (Mal. 2:4–7).

     a. God recalls His covenant with Levi while speaking with the prophet Malachi: "My covenant with him was one of life and peace."

     b. God gave Levi one of the highest affirmations of any human being in Scripture: "He feared me. He stood in awe of my name."

B. Prayer discloses our theology, so we triumphantly pray, "Thy kingdom come."

  1. Recently in the United States, societal progress promoted a postmillennial optimism, especially among liberal Protestants.

     a. Liberal Protestants believed that moral and societal progress was evidence of the incremental growth of the kingdom of God.

     b. The World Wars exposed as a false hope the assumption that the kingdom of God was growing incrementally based on progress.

     c. The failure of Protestant liberalism's view of the kingdom was its theological reduction of Christianity to a social agenda.

  2. The Lord's Prayer is kingdom-filled prayer, but the mere humanistic optimism of Protestant liberalism required a kingdom-less prayer.

     a. The Serenity Prayer, often credited to Reinhold Niebuhr, became very well known in the United States during the mid-twentieth century.

     b. A minimal prayer with a minimal theology: "God grant me the serenity to accept the things I cannot change, courage to change the things I can, and wisdom to know the difference."

  3. The Lord's Prayer and the Serenity Prayer are worlds apart theologically.

     a. The Lord's Prayer uses the first person plural; the Serenity Prayer uses the first person singular.

     b. The Lord's Prayer calls for God's kingdom to be realized; the Serenity Prayer doesn't recognize a king of a kingdom.

C. When we pray, "Thy kingdom come," we are announcing the right-now rule and reign of our Lord Jesus Christ.

  1. The Lord's Prayer is an interim prayer.

     a. Jesus inaugurated a kingdom through His life, death, burial, and resurrection—a kingdom not yet fully consummated.

     b. Regardless of the differences in eschatological views, we live in between the ascension of Jesus Christ and His imminent return.

     c. Jesus Christ will return bodily, in space and time, and set into motion a series a sequence of events that will bring the consummation of His kingdom.

  2. We must yearn for the kingdom.

a. Material comfort and safety cause us to run the risk of becoming too comfortable, such that we do not yearn for God's coming kingdom.

b. We must never forget about the real need and persecution of Christians around the world and continue to pray for the kingdom.

D. Knowing how to live out our dual citizenship is essential for hastening the kingdom.

1. Augustine spoke in terms of the city of God and the city of man to explain how Christians are to live as dual citizens.

a. The city of God is eternal, and the city of man is temporary.

b. God made the city of man for His glory and purpose, so we cannot despise the city of man.

2. The city of God and the city of man are driven by a love of its own.

a. The city of God is driven by the love of God, and the city of man is driven by the love of man—the love of self.

b. A miraculous transfer of citizenship displays God's redemptive purposes, so that people who live in the city of man love God.

3. Augustine found an answer as to how we are to live in both cities in Jesus' response to the question, "Which is the greatest commandment in the Law?"

a. Our responsibility to the city of God is "You shall love the Lord your God with all your heart and soul and mind" (Matt. 22:37).

b. Our responsibility to the city of man is "You shall love your neighbor as yourself" (Matt. 22:39).

c. We must therefore love God and be concerned for the laws, community, and happiness of the city of man.

4. Augustine understood how the problem of our sin causes us to misinterpret the city of God and assume too much of the city of man.

a. The glory of God in the triumph of the gospel can explain the delay of the fully consummated kingdom.

b. The danger of those in the city of man is to lose sight of the reality of God's coming kingdom through self-infatuation.

c. The only way to remedy this is to pray, "Thy kingdom come."

STUDY QUESTIONS

1. We will inevitably continue to pray the Lord's Prayer in heaven.
    a. True
    b. False

2. God remembers the covenant He made with _____ in Malachi 2.
    a. Abraham
    b. David
    c. Noah
    d. Levi

3. Which major twentieth-century theologian is credited with penning the Serenity Prayer?
   a. Karl Barth
   b. Paul Tillich
   c. Emil Brunner
   d. Reinhold Niebuhr

4. Liberal Protestantism was decidedly premillennial before the World Wars.
   a. True
   b. False

5. Which prominent theologian explained the Christian's dual citizenship in terms of the city of God and the city of man?
   a. Augustine
   b. Aquinas
   c. Luther
   d. Calvin

6. Dr. Mohler noted that love of man that primarily drives the city of man essentially devolves to become the love of _____ .
   a. Sin
   b. Self
   c. God
   d. Money

DISCUSSION QUESTIONS

1. How is the Serenity Prayer radically different from the Lord's Prayer? How would the life of someone who prayed the Serenity Prayer daily and the life of someone who prayed the Lord's Prayer daily be different?

2. Why does Dr. Mohler call the Lord's Prayer an interim prayer? How would you explain the gospel to someone using the second petition of the Lord's Prayer in consideration that it is an interim prayer?

3. What are some differences between the city of God and the city of man? What does the Christian life focused on the city of God look like?

4. What does the fact that God created the city of man tell you about God's purposes for it? How is this connected to the Lord's Prayer?

6

Thy Word Be Done

INTRODUCTION

To pray, "Thy kingdom come," we must know what God's kingdom is and how He wills to bring it about. In this lesson, Dr. Mohler defines God's kingdom, following the progression of the Lord's Prayer into the third petition, "Thy will be done."

LESSON OBJECTIVES

1. To define the kingdom of God for whose coming Jesus taught us to pray
2. To address the confusion about the will of God related to His kingdom

SCRIPTURE READING

And your house and your kingdom shall be made sure forever before me. Your throne shall be established forever.

—2 Samuel 7:16

Do not be conformed to this world, but be transformed by the renewal of your mind, that by testing you may discern what is the will of God, what is good and acceptable and perfect.

—Romans 12:2

LECTURE OUTLINE

A. The Lord's Prayer, particularly in the second and third petitions, is deeply subversive to any earthly authority that does not govern in accordance with God's will.

    1. Many earthly rulers fear when Christians pray, "Thy kingdom come," from the Roman Empire to the Communist Party in China.

    2. The biblical worldview embraces government as a gift; in fact, anarchy is one of the worst calamities that can befall a people in the Bible (Num. 16).

   a. Paul and Peter assign a clear responsibility to government and remind us
       of our responsibility to government (Rom. 13:1–7; 1 Peter 2:13–17).
   b. The Bible also gives us examples such as Daniel and his friends who
       refused to worship idols or bow down to earthly rulers.

B. When we pray, "Thy kingdom come," we are praying for a specially defined
    kingdom.

   1. Graeme Goldsworthy defined the kingdom of God as "God's people living in
       God's place under God's rule and blessing."
   2. "God's rule" is an important phrase to note in Goldsworthy's definition.
       a. "God's rule" reminds us that a hallmark of the kingdom of God will be
           obedience to Him.
       b. Obedience to God marks out God's people; the only way a Christian's life
           can be explained is the transforming power of the gospel.
   3. "God's place" is another important phrase to note in Goldsworthy's definition.
       a. The kingdom is present right now in the church, where God's people will-
           ingly submit to God's rule in obedience and faith.
       b. The church exists in the dimensions of the "already but not yet," but God's
           kingdom is an eternal kingdom.
       c. God's place is thus an eternal place, a new heaven and new earth where
           Christ sits enthroned forever (2 Sam. 7:8–17; Rev. 11:15).

C. Praying for a specially defined kingdom naturally leads to praying for the specially
    designated way of ushering in that kingdom.

   1. Liberal Protestants and some evangelicals have confused the means chosen by
       God to bring about the kingdom.
       a. Liberal Protestants have believed that social progress is the way to usher
           in the kingdom of God.
       b. Evangelicals have believed that political action and cultural influence are
           the way to usher in the kingdom of God.
   2. Preaching the Word of God is the only way to usher in the kingdom of God.
       a. Philip Ryken said, "The only way people come into God's kingdom is by
           hearing His heralds proclaim a crucified King."
       b. "Thy kingdom come" is translated into action through obedience in the
           preaching of God's Word, evangelism, missions, and church planting.
   3. Praying for God's kingdom obligates us to pray for God's will.
       a. The city of God and the city of man are present in the third petition of the
           Lord's Prayer, "Thy will be done, on earth as it is in heaven."
       b. The love of God and the love of neighbor, as the governing principle for
           those who are citizens of both cities, are present as well.
   4. Christ has given the church the keys of the kingdom (Matt. 16:13–20).
       a. The kingdom is manifested by the church, so in rightly declaring the gos-
           pel we are ushering in God's kingdom according to His will.

b. Through the preaching of the Word and the ordinary means of grace, the church is the visible sign of the future kingdom.

D. The notion of finding the will of God is a modern misconception concerning God's sovereignty that has never been a significant theme in the history of the church.

1. The modern parlance of finding God's will contains dangerous assumptions.

a. It assumes that a special key is needed to unlock God's hidden will, and that we may be unwilling once God's will is found.

b. These assumptions misunderstand God's sovereignty and how He ordinarily works to guide us and to create in us willing hearts.

2. We can discern God's will by ordinary circumstances and the Word.

a. Christian vocation was a great insight of the Reformation, prominent in Martin Luther's theology, that recovered the teaching that every Christian has a calling.

b. Christian vocation reveals itself in life's ordinary circumstances, in which we are to live by the wisdom of God's Word.

3. Romans 12:1–2 is a classic text on Christian obedience that defines the will of God as good, acceptable, and perfect.

a. God's will is good because God is good; His purpose for our lives is good no matter what His will for our lives is.

b. God's will is acceptable, so we should embrace it when it is revealed in our circumstances and supported in His Word for His glory.

c. God's will is perfect, and thus He will demonstrate His perfection through it for all to see when His kingdom is consummated.

STUDY QUESTIONS

1. A biblical worldview acknowledges government as a necessary burden.
    a. True
    b. False

2. The rebellion of _____ was used as an example of the calamities that befall people in a state of anarchy.
    a. Ananias
    b. Nadab
    c. Korah
    d. Ham

3. Who defined the kingdom of God as "God's people living in God's place under God's rule and blessing"?
    a. Graeme Goldsworthy
    b. Reinhold Niebuhr
    c. Roger Scruton
    d. Philip Ryken

4. Christians throughout the ages have been fascinated with discovering God's will for their lives.
    a. True
    b. False

5. The subject of Christian vocation was prevalent in the theology of which theologian?
    a. Calvin
    b. Luther
    c. Aquinas
    d. Augustine

6. Andrew Fuller said that God's will is "worthy of _____."
    a. Affection
    b. Adoration
    c. Adaptation
    d. Acceptance

DISCUSSION QUESTIONS

1. Why would earthly authorities consider Christianity subversive? In what way is a Christian's understanding of civil government misunderstood? Can you think of any historical examples for support?

2. What are liberal Protestants' (and even some evangelicals') common misconceptions about manifesting God's kingdom on earth? Can you identify the common problem shared by these methods?

3. If someone told you about their desire to know God's will for their life, how would you help them to see the problems embedded in their theology?

4. Where is the kingdom of God visibly present today? What are some ways you know this to be true?

7

Presence of the Kingdom

INTRODUCTION

God's kingdom will be consummated on His terms, according to the perfection of His will. In this lesson, Dr. Mohler corrects misconceptions concerning the will of God so that we might pray in a way that truly honors Him.

LESSON OBJECTIVES

1. To demonstrate how God's kingdom and will are absolutely sovereign
2. To expose and correct theological errors concerning the will of God

SCRIPTURE READING

As for you, you meant evil against me, but God meant it for good, to bring it about that many people should be kept alive, as they are today.

—Genesis 50:20

The secret things belong to the Lord our God, but the things that are revealed belong to us and to our children forever.

—Deuteronomy 29:29a

This Jesus, delivered up according to the definite plan and foreknowledge of God, you crucified and killed by the hands of lawless men.

—Acts 2:23

LECTURE OUTLINE

A. Declaring the kingdom of God is countercultural, because God's rule is absolute.

1. Most people have lived under the reign of a king or a queen throughout the span of human history.

a. World War I marked the end of many powerful empires, but despite this, people still have a strong, residual understanding of kingdoms.

b. Today, kingdoms are subtle, and the principalities and powers are far more numerous than we often acknowledge.

2. Many contemporary people are resistant to kings and kingdoms.

a. George Arthur Butterick captured modern sentiments by saying, "When you say the word 'kingdom,' it smacks of totalitarianism."

b. People are resistant to kings and kingdoms because they do not want to live under anyone's rule.

c. Kings, by definition, rule over the subjects of their kingdom; therefore, declaring the kingdom of God is countercultural.

B. Just as God's rule is absolute over all of creation, God's will is absolutely indivisible.

1. Misunderstanding God's will leads to a misunderstanding of God's gospel.

a. God has one will, and positing that God has multiple wills causes problems and even influences the way people share the gospel.

b. The indivisible nature of God's will means that the gospel should never be presented as if it were God's alternative plan.

c. Redemption through Jesus Christ was God's predetermined plan to be worked out according to His sovereign will (Acts 2:23; 4:28).

2. Leslie Weatherhead created a threefold description of God's will that has negatively influenced many Christians.

a. Weatherhead believed that God has three wills: an intentional will, a contingent or permissive will, and an ultimate will.

b. Weatherhead believed that God will accomplish His ultimate will, but God's permissive will was the only way to explain the state of our world.

c. Weatherhead created divisions in order explain the existence of evil, but Scripture doesn't create divisions within the will of God.

C. John Calvin and Martin Luther faithfully described the will of God.

1. Calvin argued that God never merely permits anything.

a. God is sovereign, so the category of "permission" is not helpful, because as sovereign, God is responsible for what He permits.

b. B.B. Warfield said, "If God is the author of the cosmos . . . then He's responsible for everything that follows."

2. Calvin's theology allowed him to write, "God permitted this to happen," to people he was encouraging during the Protestant Reformation.

a. Calvin did not contradict himself; he understood that whenever we speak of God as permitting something to happen, we can simultaneously affirm that God ordained it.

b. Permission, in this sense, does not mean that God merely allowed something that He could not have prevented to happen, as Weatherhead's theology teaches.

3. Calvin's understanding of God's will honors God's sovereignty.
   a. God ordained His triumph over evil to showcase the surpassing glory of His name.
   b. God ordained the fall in order to reveal Himself to us as both Creator and Redeemer.
4. Luther spoke about the will of God in terms of God's left and right hand.
   a. God's right hand is His revealed will, which He has revealed to us in His Word, and God's left hand is His inscrutable will, which He did not.
   b. Christians must simultaneously confess the sovereign goodness of God and the inscrutability of His ways.

D. Open theism developed as a way of dealing with the problem of evil and suffering, but its theological presumptions corrode the core of the Christian faith.
   1. Open theism gained a showing in evangelical institutions during the 1980s and the 1990s.
   2. Open theism's central premise is that God's foreknowledge is limited to that which can be known.
      a. The underlying presupposition above is the preservation of human freedom, which is at the cost of God's sovereignty and omniscience.
      b. With free will at the center of its theological system, open theism is the logical conclusion of Arminianism applied to the doctrine of God.
      c. Open theism's attempt to solve the problem of evil undermines a foundational confidence in God.
   3. The Lord's Prayer is not a prayer of mere hopefulness; it is a prayer of confidence that the kingdom has already been inaugurated.
      a. When we pray, "on earth as it is in heaven," we pray for what is already true in heaven to be manifested on earth.
      b. God's kingdom is manifested on earth; we see it displayed in our churches and families.

STUDY QUESTIONS

1. John Calvin made fine distinctions within the will of God.
   a. True
   b. False

2. George Arthur Butterick captured the modern distaste for authority when he said, "When you say the word 'kingdom,' it smacks of _____."
   a. Hatred
   b. Tyranny
   c. Oppression
   d. Totalitarianism

3. Understanding that God only has one will is tied to which of His attributes?
    a. Aseity
    b. Eternality
    c. Indivisibility
    d. Immateriality

4. The theological foundation of open theism is shared with Arminianism.
    a. True
    b. False

5. Leslie Weatherhead distorted God's will by dividing it into an intentional, ultimate, and a contingent will, which is also called God's _____ will.
    a. Decretive
    b. Preceptive
    c. Permissive
    d. Declarative

6. _____ said, "If God is the author of the cosmos . . . then He's responsible for everything that follows."
    a. George Arthur Butterick
    b. Leslie Weatherhead
    c. B.B. Warfield
    d. John Calvin

DISCUSSION QUESTIONS

1. Using historical and contemporary examples, what are some of the reasons that make declaring the kingdom of God countercultural?

2. In what ways can Christians distort the will of God in relation to the gospel? How would such a distortion detract from God's glory in terms of who He is and what He has done for you in Christ?

3. How is open theism the logical consequence of Arminianism? How could these theologies work to undermine a Christian's confidence?

4. What makes Leslie Weatherhead's understanding of the will of God and John Calvin's understanding of the will of God so different? How could Calvin say, "God permitted this to happen," and still be consistent?

8

Daily Dependence

INTRODUCTION

God has given us bread as a daily reminder of our need for Him. In this lesson, Dr. Mohler traces a biblical theology of bread throughout the Bible, discovering that our deepest hungers can only be filled by Jesus Christ, the Bread of Life.

LESSON OBJECTIVES

1. To approach the daily need for bread from a biblical-theological standpoint
2. To advance our focus beyond our daily material needs to Jesus Christ

SCRIPTURE READING

Come, everyone who thirsts, come to the waters; and he who has no money, come, buy and eat!

—Isaiah 55:1a

I am the living bread that came down from heaven. If anyone eats of this bread, he will live forever. And the bread that I will give for the life of the world is my flesh.

—John 6:51

LECTURE OUTLINE

A. A biblical theology of bread points to our daily need and dependence on God.

　1. When we pray, "Give us this day our daily bread," we recognize our dependence on God.

　　a. We should never hesitate to ask God for the necessities of life, because God created us to be dependent on Him.

　　b. God alone is self-sufficient; we are His creatures, created in His image for His glory and utterly dependent on Him.

      c. Our neediness is on display every time we glance at an utterly dependent and defenseless baby.

  2. Our need for sustenance and nutrition is a universal need.

      a. A massive percentage of advertising and a large part of our everyday life is devoted to food—an amazingly uniform, cross-culture reality.

      b. Secular evolutionary thought believes the human need for sustenance and nutrition is a deficiency in the evolutionary process.

      c. Biblical Christian thought understands that God gave us the need for sustenance and nutrition as a reminder that we are not self-sufficient.

  3. Our need for sustenance and nutrition is a daily need.

      a. The phrase commonly translated, "daily bread," is a notoriously difficult word to translate from the Greek.

      b. William Tyndale coined the phrase "daily bread" in his English translation of the Bible to convey the sense of the Greek.

B. A biblical theology of bread points out the nature of our dependence in a fallen world.

  1. Our hunger is not a result of the fall, but the fact that people go hungry for lack of food is evidence of the fall.

      a. Adam and Eve needed sustenance and nutrition in the garden of Eden—the necessity of sustenance and nutrition is part of creation.

      b. God has amply provided for us in His creation, so the reality of poverty and world hunger must be attributed to our sin.

  2. The understanding that poverty and world hunger do not stem from mere food shortage has become more prevalent in the twenty-first century.

      a. Christians understand that the problem of world hunger fundamentally stems from the reality of sin.

      b. Secular recognition that people are to blame for the inadequate distribution of food is a step further from deflecting blame to a scarcity of resources.

  3. The wilderness wandering of the children of Israel graphically depicts our daily need and dependence on God's faithful provision.

      a. Israel wandered in the wilderness for forty years; God was barring the first generation from the Promised Land because of their unbelief.

      b. The children of the first generation would enter the Promised Land but only after being sustained in the wilderness by God's provision.

      c. God provided for Israel in a way they could never have provided for themselves in the wilderness by giving them manna from heaven.

      d. Israel experienced salvation from certain starvation by God's daily provision of manna to remind them of their dependence on Him.

  4. Israel's propensity to forget about their dependence on God is a temptation for modern Christians in the West.

      a. We may not know what it is like to read about manna from heaven or pray the Lord's Prayer with a deep awareness of our daily need.

b. The Lord's Prayer should be our constant acknowledgement that we are dependent upon God—our daily sustenance is God's gift.

c. Thankfulness should lead us to pray in solidarity and communion for everyone around the world who is in desperate need of daily bread.

C. A biblical theology of bread points beyond our daily material needs to Jesus Christ.

1. Jesus' wilderness experience parallels Israel's wilderness experience and reveals how our hunger can be satisfied spiritually.

a. Israel was in the wilderness grumbling; Jesus was in the wilderness praying and fasting.

b. Jesus, as true Israel, demonstrated His obedience and dependence on the Father by resisting Satan.

c. Jesus answered Satan, "Man shall not live by bread alone, but by every word that comes from the mouth of God" (Matt. 4:4).

d. Jesus' response reveals our ultimate dependence upon and obedience to God.

2. Jesus is the Bread of Life, sent from heaven, given for the life of the world.

a. One of the powerful "I am" statements from the gospel of John: "I am the bread of life" (John 6:48).

b. We must yearn for bread that leads to far more than mere sustenance and nutrition and yearn for bread that leads to everlasting life.

STUDY QUESTIONS

1. The petition "Give us this day our daily bread" should make us question our supposed self-sufficiency.
    a. True
    b. False

2. "Daily bread" was a phrase originally coined in whose translation of Scripture?
    a. Luther's
    b. Jerome's
    c. Erasmus'
    d. Tyndale's

3. A biblical-theological approach to praying for daily bread should cause us to remember which of the following?
    a. Israel
    b. Adam
    c. Jesus
    d. All of the above

4. World hunger stems from what fundamental problem?
    a. Food shortage
    b. The reality of sin
    c. The inadequate distribution of food
    d. The greed of First World countries

5. "I am the bread of life" is one of the many "I am" statements characteristic of whose gospel?
    a. Matthew's
    b. Mark's
    c. Luke's
    d. John's

6. The people of Israel among the generation that would enter the Promised Land are called "_____ ones" throughout the book of Deuteronomy.
    a. Holy
    b. Little
    c. Faithful
    d. Chosen

DISCUSSION QUESTIONS

1. Why did Dr. Mohler trace a biblical theology of bread throughout the storyline of the Bible?

2. In what way does God display the reality of our dependence upon Him in His works of creation and redemption?

3. How can Christians who are not worried about where their next meal will come from pray for daily bread with similar urgency?

4. How is Jesus' experience in the wilderness unlike Israel's experience in the wilderness? What does Jesus' response to Satan when tempted to turn stones into bread reveal about God's purposes for us?

9

Forgiven & Forgiving

INTRODUCTION

Jesus Christ has freed us from the debt of our sin, and because of that, we must freely forgive others. In this lesson, Dr. Mohler develops the idea of debt as a picture of our sin, pointing toward the heart of the Christian faith—forgiveness.

LESSON OBJECTIVES

1. To evaluate the variations on the fifth petition of the Lord's Prayer
2. To emphasize the correspondence between being forgiven and being forgiving

SCRIPTURE READING

Let us then with confidence draw near to the throne of grace, that we may receive mercy and find grace to help in time of need.

—Hebrews 4:16

If we confess our sins, he is faithful and just to forgive us our sins and to cleanse us from all unrighteousness.

—1 John 1:9

LECTURE OUTLINE

A. We should pray, "Forgive us our debts," and not merely, "Forgive us our trespasses."
   1. "Trespass" does not adequately address the problem of sin; in one sense, it is appropriate, but in another sense, it makes our sin sound accidental.
   2. Substituting "trespasses" for "debts" fails to capitalize on our knowledge of debt as an ever-growing problem.
      a. Debt has been a problem throughout history, but most recently it has become more acceptable, even in cultures influenced by Christianity.

        b.   Christians have always understood that debt should be avoided at all costs because it places one in the vulnerable position of debtor.

        c.   Christians developed this understanding because the Bible speaks of debt as if it were a type of prison.

  3. Prisons in a modern American context significantly differ from prison during the time of the Roman Empire.

        a.   Because of our modern understanding of incarceration, we commonly think of a prison as a place someone goes to pay off a debt to society.

        b.   The prisons of the Roman Empire were not filled with criminals, because criminals were subjected to different types of punishment.

        c.   Debtors were the only people with long-term prison sentences, which were often used to leverage the repayment of debt.

  4. The fact that Jesus taught His disciples to pray, "Forgive us our debts," would have been shocking within the context of the Roman Empire.

        a.   If praying, "Forgive us our debts," does not shock us, then we have become all too familiar with debt.

        b.   The last words of Martin Luther perfectly capture our indebtedness: "We are beggars. This is true."

B. "Forgive us our debts" informs us of our need to be forgiven and the reality that forgiveness is available for our sins.

  1. The fifth petition establishes that we are debtors in need of forgiveness.

        a.   We are debtors because the penalty for our sins is much greater than we could ever pay, but Jesus paid the debt of our sin on the cross.

        b.   Jesus accomplished even more than paying our debt, which is why the atonement cannot be reduced to one metaphor.

  2. The fifth petition establishes the reality of forgiveness and reinforces the knowledge of our sin.

        a.   The Lord's Prayer is a confident prayer, because we pray knowing that we can approach God because of what Jesus has done for us.

        b.   The One who saves us from our sin is the One who taught us to pray, "Forgive us our debts, as we also forgive our debtors."

        c.   The fifth petition forces us to acknowledge our sin so that we can bring it before God; otherwise, we make Him a liar (1 John 1:8–9).

C. "As we also have forgiven our debtors" informs us that those who are forgiven are those who are forgiving.

  1. Jesus warned the disciples about distortions that lead people to believe that they are religiously superior to others.

        a.   Truly understanding God's forgiveness toward you naturally leads to a disposition of forgiveness toward others.

        b.   Christians are the forgiven and must also be the forgiving.

2. Jesus taught us that we must forgive others from our heart (Matt. 18:21–35).
   a. Jesus answered Peter's question "Lord, how often will my brother sin against me, and I forgive him?" without giving a number; we must forgive perfectly.
   b. The parable of the unforgiving servant, which follows Peter's question, pictures the reality that the unforgiven are the unforgiving.
   c. The way we forgive others evidences our salvation, that we have truly experienced the grace and mercy of God.
3. God is faithful to forgive us when we pray for forgiveness.
   a. We should ask the Lord to forgive us our debts because in Christ our debt has already been canceled—God has settled the matter.
   b. A declaration of forgiveness follows the prayer of confession in worship because the gospel itself is the declaration of forgiveness.
4. The Lord's Prayer requires strategic, gospel-minded thinking.
   a. We must keep an inventory of our sins in order to confess as well as an inventory of what we must forgive.
   b. The Lord's Prayer will transform your prayer life and help you to answer the question, "How forgiving are you?"

STUDY QUESTIONS

1. "Forgive us our trespasses" is more common in a Roman Catholic context.
   a. True
   b. False

2. Martin Luther mixed German with what other language as he slipped in and out of consciousness in his final hour?
   a. Hebrew
   b. French
   c. Greek
   d. Latin

3. "Trespasses" can make sin sound _____ .
   a. Extreme
   b. Grievous
   c. Accidental
   d. None of the above

4. Jesus answered the question, "Lord, how often will my brother sin against me, and I forgive him?" with a number.
   a. True
   b. False

5. Throughout the Gospels, who is often the spokesman for the Apostles?
    a. Matthew
    b. James
    c. Peter
    d. John

6. Our own familiarity with _____ makes the Lord's Prayer less shocking to us than it would have been to the disciples.
    a. Forgiveness
    b. Christ
    c. Debt
    d. Sin

DISCUSSION QUESTIONS

1. Dr. Mohler argued that "debt" is a stronger word to use in the Lord's Prayer than "trespasses." What do you think are the advantages and disadvantages of these words?

2. What do you think is the most important implication of this fifth petition of the Lord's Prayer?

3. How was debt thought of differently in a first-century context than it is today?

4. What is the greatest question you must ask yourself when praying the fifth petition of the Lord's Prayer? How would you answer?

10

Cause Us to Flee

INTRODUCTION

Temptation is a fact of life in this fallen world, even for the most faithful believers. In this lesson, Dr. Mohler clarifies what it means to ask the Father not to lead us into temptation and distinguishes the differences between trials and temptations.

LESSON OBJECTIVES

1. To emphasize the never-ceasing danger of temptation in the Christian life
2. To explain the sixth petition of the Lord's Prayer by clarifying language and differentiating between tests and temptations

SCRIPTURE READING

Watch and pray that you may not enter into temptation.

—Matthew 26:41a

God is faithful, and he will not let you be tempted beyond your ability, but with the temptation he will also provide the way of escape, that you may be able to endure it.

—1 Corinthians 10:13b

LECTURE OUTLINE

A. Temptation is an ever-present reality.
  1. The beginning pages of Scripture reveal that temptation is a serious threat.
    a. In Genesis 4:7, God warns Cain that sin is crouching at the door and that he must rule over it before it rules over him.
    b. Since the fall, temptation is a reality with which we must live; it is dangerous, especially when we fail to recognize it.
  2. Sin's desire to rule over us is exactly why we pray, "Thy kingdom come, thy will be done on earth as it is in heaven."

      a. When we pray the Lord's Prayer, we are praying that God's rule will conquer our lives so that sin will not have dominion over us.

      b. The picture of sin crouching at the door is descriptive of our battle with temptation, a battle that shouldn't be spoken of frivolously or glorified.

B. The language of the Lord's Prayer requires that we make a distinction between tests and temptation, because God doesn't tempt us—He tests us.

    1. "Lead us not into temptation" is shepherding language.

      a. God is not the author of evil, so He does not lead us into temptation; He cannot be blamed for our sin.

      b. We pray, "Lead us not into temptation," because God is our Shepherd, and He leads His flock away from danger.

      c. We have no reason to worry that God would ever lead us astray but every reason to trust that we will be led on the right path.

    2. The Bible makes clear that God tests but never tempts; the classic text to prove this is found in Genesis 22 with the testing of Abraham.

      a. Modern people are often repulsed by this passage of Scripture; it is viewed as immoral and as grounds for questioning God's character.

      b. Despite modern views of this passage, Scripture reveals Abraham's faith in God's provision and promise (Gen. 22:8).

      c. Hebrews 11:17–18 affirms that Abraham prevailed in the faith while being tested, believing that God would raise Isaac from the dead.

      d. Abraham believed in God's power to fulfill His covenantal promises in Isaac, pointing to the ultimate fulfillment in the resurrection of Christ.

C. Making a distinction between tests and temptations informs how we ought to pray.

    1. Trials and tribulations are a part of the Christian life, so we do not pray for God to stop testing us, but we do pray that we not succumb to temptation.

    2. Christ's incarnate experience of temptation in the wilderness further directs our prayer upward, in confidence amid temptation, to the throne of grace.

      a. God the Father, by His Spirit, led His own Son into a test to be tempted by Satan, undertaking temptation on our behalf.

      b. Christ's temptations have direct ramifications on His role as our High Priest, who identifies with us in our temptations, without sin (Heb. 4:15).

      c. When we experience temptation, we can approach Jesus Christ as our merciful Savior to experience His love and refuge.

    3. The reality of tests and temptations should not cause us to lose heart, for we must be joyful as God purposes to work through them (James 1:2–4).

    4. The reality of temptation should cause us to pray urgently, in full recognition of the dangers of temptation.

      a. Despite the contemporary misconception that the world is a safe place, we live in a dangerous world of snares and temptations.

    b. Christians should not expect to escape temptation at any point in this life; so long as we are in the world, sin is crouching at the door.

5. The Lord's Prayer reinforces our need to run from the temptation to sin as we pray, never rationalizing or looking back.

STUDY QUESTIONS

1. The Father tempted Jesus Christ by leading Him into the wilderness.
    a. True
    b. False

2. When thinking about temptation, it is important to remember that "sin is _____ at the door."
    a. Lurking
    b. Waiting
    c. Knocking
    d. Crouching

3. Modern people tend to think that the testing of Abraham is _____ .
    a. Immoral
    b. Repulsive
    c. Perplexing
    d. All of the above

4. Christians can escape temptation by reaching a state of spiritual maturity.
    a. True
    b. False

5. According to the author of Hebrews, Abraham's faith in God as exhibited in Genesis 22 supports which doctrine?
    a. Resurrection
    b. Incarnation
    c. Atonement
    d. Trinity

6. The sixth petition of the Lord's Prayer, "Lead us not into temptation," should primarily be understood as what kind of language?
    a. Analogical
    b. Shepherding
    c. Archaic
    d. Biblical

DISCUSSION QUESTIONS

1. How would you explain the difference between God's testing someone and the false notion of God's tempting someone? What examples from the Bible would help support your argument?

2. How does the world trivialize and glorify temptation? What does God's warning to Cain tell you about the danger of being worldly minded concerning temptation?

3. Imagine you are praying using the Lord's Prayer as an outline. What are some possible prayers that would effectively incorporate the implications of Christ's temptations on your Christian life?

4. How have your struggles against sin and temptation changed as you have grown and matured in the Christian faith? How have they not changed?

11

A Desperate Plea

INTRODUCTION

In God's sovereign hand, our trials and temptations are not without purpose. In this lesson, Dr. Mohler points us to our hope amid such difficulties, that God is using them in this world of sin, evil, and death to His glorious ends.

LESSON OBJECTIVES

1. To explain God's powerful purpose behind our trials and temptations
2. To equip Christians with the necessary principles to resist temptation

SCRIPTURE READING

Count it all joy, my brothers, when you meet trials of various kings, for you know that the testing of you faith produces steadfastness.

—James 1:2–3

LECTURE OUTLINE

A. When we pray, "Lead us not into temptation," we acquire a thoughtfulness necessary for living in the world, enduring our trials, and preparing our children.

1. The Lord's Prayer reminds us that we are living in a dangerous world.
   a. The comforts of modern life can make it difficult for us to read Scripture as faithfully as we ought.
   b. We must read Scripture carefully, especially during times of peace and prosperity, in order to understand the world in which we live.
2. The Lord's Prayer forces us to acknowledge the purpose behind our trials.
   a. James 1:2–4 is explicit: our trials are a reason to be joyful because through them God is perfecting our faith to the fullness of maturity.
   b. Rejoicing in trials is difficult, but how we endure every aspect of our trials is the determining factor of faithfulness vs. unfaithfulness.

        c. We must rejoice in our trials because they will produce steadfastness, which will further prove to us our faith.

        d. We must not escape our trials but allow steadfastness to have its full effect and develop in us virtues we may never have had otherwise.

    3. The Lord's Prayer helps us to see the importance of preparing our children.

        a. Christians are called to raise their children in the nurture and admonition of the Lord (Eph. 6:4).

        b. Responsibly raising our children as commanded is important for when they face trials so that their faithfulness can emerge out of them.

        c. We need trials just as much as our children do to develop our skills and character so that God can prepare us for future service.

B. Christian principles are necessary for navigating through our temptations.

    1. We must recognize that temptations are a daily threat to our life with Christ.

        a. Christians are not immune to temptation; believing otherwise can only lead us into danger.

        b. We must never cease in praying for the grace of the gospel expressed in our union with Christ and the power of His indwelling Spirit.

    2. We must understand that temptation cannot be resisted by our own power.

        a. Sheer willpower cannot help us to effectively war against temptation; in fact, our wills are not as strong as we think.

        b. The notion of willpower is prevalent in our society, but we cannot elevate human will beyond how it is characterized in Scripture.

        c. Temptation is our default position; the will does not interrupt the process of going from a neutral state to a state of temptation.

        d. We are absolutely vulnerable to temptation apart from God, who empowers us in Christ and surrounds us in Christian fellowship.

    3. We must pray for endurance in the fight against temptation because the fight against sin is a lifelong battle.

    4. We must pray that the Lord will deliver us from our own personal individual patterns of temptation.

        a. Every Christian has different patterns of temptation, so we must guard against our particular patterns of temptation.

        b. We must pray against our patterns of sin, that the indwelling Christ would work in us to make us love what we would otherwise not love.

C. God's saving work in the gospel and the real presence of evil in the world are implied when we pray, "Lead us not into temptation, but deliver us from evil."

    1. The Lord's Prayer is a plea for God's sovereign deliverance.

        a. Deliverance from temptation is no different than deliverance in the gospel; God delivers us monergistically.

        b. A synergistic gospel is no gospel at all because there is nothing we can do to rescue ourselves.

  c. When we pray the Lord's Prayer, we are asking God to rescue us, and in being rescued, we are by definition rescued by another.

2. Christianity fully acknowledges the real presence of evil in the world.

  a. A truly Christian worldview explains the existence of evil and announces its defeat; it doesn't deny it as Christian Science does.

  b. Scripture frankly acknowledges the evil of death, our final foe; this is illustrated in Jesus' weeping over Lazarus' death (John 11:35; 1 Cor. 15).

  c. Scripture frankly acknowledges moral evil—the evil we commit—as well as natural evil—the evil that is a part of a corrupted world.

STUDY QUESTIONS

1. We faithfully pray, "Deliver us from evil," from a synergistic point of view.
  a. True
  b. False

2. Temptation is not a _____ threat for mature Christians.
  a. Dangerous
  b. Significant
  c. Passing
  d. Daily

3. What is an unhelpful category under which to think about temptation?
  a. Grace
  b. Depravity
  c. Willpower
  d. Sanctification

4. Natural evil is the type of evil we naturally commit.
  a. True
  b. False

5. The shortest verse of the Bible directly confronts which reality?
  a. Sin
  b. Evil
  c. Death
  d. Satan

6. A biblically based worldview takes evil seriously, unlike the unscriptural worldview of _____, founder of Christian Science.
  a. Joseph Smith
  b. Ellen G. White
  c. Mary Baker Eddy
  d. Charles Taze Russell

DISCUSSION QUESTIONS

1. Dr. Mohler presented four principles for Christians to remember about tempta-
    tion. Summarize these principles. Which one did you find most helpful? Why?

2. What are some of the trials through which God has delivered you? How are you a
    different person because of them?

3. How could the illusion of modern safety and comfort distort the way we read
    Scripture? How must we read Scripture appropriately in light of Dr. Mohler's
    lecture?

4. How is asking for deliverance in the Lord's Prayer a picture of salvation in Jesus
    Christ? How does this encourage you to count your trials as joy?

12

Forever Victorious

INTRODUCTION

Christians have an adversary, a reality we have to face, but not apart from the reality of his defeat. In this lesson, Dr. Mohler explains how the devil's defeat is one of the reasons why we rightly conclude the Lord's Prayer with a doxology.

LESSON OBJECTIVES

1. To affirm the existence and announce the defeat of the evil one
2. To build a case in support of the doxological ending of the Lord's Prayer

SCRIPTURE READING

Yours, O Lord, is the greatest and the power and the glory and the victory and the majesty, for all that is in the heavens and in the earth is yours. Yours is the kingdom, O Lord, and you are exalted as head over all.

—1 Chronicles 29:11

LECTURE OUTLINE

A. The Christian worldview not only affirms the existence of evil but also the existence of an evil one, an evil one who has already been defeated by Jesus Christ.

1. The glorious announcement of Christ's victory affirms the reality of evil.
   a. The promise of Christ's victory over evil first appears in Genesis 3:15 with the promise that He would crush the serpent's head.
   b. Both the promise and the fulfillment of the promise remind us of the fundamental truth that we must pray to be delivered from evil.
2. There is only one biblical way to view Satan's role and power.
   a. Some can go so far as to deny the reality of an evil one, and others can go so far as to have an imbalanced obsession with the evil one.

47

      b.   The Bible clearly affirms the devil's existence and the devil's defeat, so his existence and his defeat must be acknowledged.

B. First Peter 5:8–11 speaks candidly about the devil, his defeat, and how we resist him.

    1. Satan seeks to destroy Christians in order to nullify the promises of the gospel of Christ, but we can stand firm in the promises of God.

      a. We cannot demythologize the devil—he exists, and because he exists, we can know that temptation continually surrounds us.

      b. Christ has triumphed over sin, death, and the devil; we only must endure in the power of the Spirit for "a little while" (1 Peter 5:10).

    2. We must resist the devil by standing firm in Christ's victory and God's Word.

      a. The most subversive question ever to undercut the authority of God's Word was asked by the serpent in the garden: "Did God actually say?"

      b. Jesus underwent the same line of questioning as our first parents in His wilderness temptations, undergoing temptation for us.

      c. When we resist the devil, we not only look at Christ's victory over him at the cross but also Christ's victory over him in temptation.

      d. The Word of God is the only offensive weapon we have to war against the devil (Eph. 6:10–20).

      e. We must keep Scripture in our hearts and our minds when resisting the devil, proclaiming of his defeat in the name of Christ.

    3. Peter ends his letter with a doxology, as is appropriately common in the Lord's Prayer: "To him be the dominion forever and ever. Amen."

C. The Lord's Prayer should be concluded on the victorious note: "For thine is the kingdom, and the power, and the glory forever. Amen."

    1. The absence of the doxology in ancient manuscripts raises the question as to whether it is appropriate to add to the end of the Lord's Prayer.

      a. The doxology is absent from all ancient Latin manuscripts though it is present in almost all ancient Greek manuscripts.

      b. According to an analysis of the New Testament textual history, Jesus ended the Lord's Prayer in the way found in most modern translations.

      c. The presence of the doxology in Greek manuscripts reveals that the early church prayed the Lord's Prayer with the doxology nonetheless.

    2. Appending a doxology to the Lord's Prayer is appropriate and supported by Scripture and tradition.

      a. Appending a doxology to the Lord's Prayer would be wrong if we did it with the intention of adding to Scripture.

      b. Jesus never commanded us to pray the Lord's Prayer exclusively; appending a doxology to it is a fitting declaration of God's glory.

      c. Prayers in the Old Testament, especially in the Psalms, end in a doxology, so the doxology of the Lord's Prayer has scriptural warrant.

d. The Lord's Prayer in the *Didache*—one of the most ancient forms of Christian teaching—ends in almost the exact same doxology.

3. The doxology of the Lord's Prayer covers the theological range of the content of the Lord's Prayer, so it is an appropriate addition to the Lord's Prayer.

  a. "For thine is the kingdom"—Jesus taught us to pray for the coming kingdom and the perfect will of God to be done on earth.

  b. "And the power"—Jesus taught us to pray for God's power to provide us with daily bread, forgiveness, and deliverance.

  c. "And the glory"—Jesus taught us to pray for God's name to be hallowed.

STUDY QUESTIONS

1. The armor of God described by Paul in Ephesians 6 is entirely defensive.
  a. True
  b. False

2. Dr. Mohler remarked how important it is to remember Christ's _____ temptation when resisting the devil.
  a. Exemplary
  b. Substitutionary
  c. Satisfactory
  d. Influential

3. Dr. Mohler borrowed the term "_____" from twentieth-century Protestant liberalism to describe the denial of the devil's existence.
  a. Disavow
  b. Demystify
  c. Disconfirm
  d. Demythologize

4. The doxology traditionally added to the Lord's Prayer is present in almost all of the ancient Greek manuscripts.
  a. True
  b. False

5. An argument in support of the doxology traditionally added to the Lord's Prayer can be made from the doxologies found in the _____ .
  a. Psalms
  b. Didache
  c. Old Testament
  d. All of the above

6. Which theme in the doxology is also represented in the rest of the Lord's Prayer?
   a. God's kingdom
   b. God's power
   c. God's holy name
   d. All of the above

DISCUSSION QUESTIONS

1. What are some important things to remember for resisting the devil? How would these be helpful to someone who is overly fascinated with the demonic or someone who denies Satan's influence?

2. What has been Satan's primary point of attack throughout the narrative of the Bible from the garden of Eden to the wilderness temptations of Christ? Why do you think Satan is so focused on attacking this one area?

3. Dr. Mohler argued for the appropriateness of the doxology traditionally added to the end of the Lord's Prayer. What was the most convincing point of Dr. Mohler's argument? Why?

4. Have you committed the Lord's Prayer to memory? If so, how has this helped your prayer life? If not, what have these lessons taught you about the benefits of praying the way Jesus taught us to pray?

ANSWER KEY FOR STUDY QUESTIONS

Lesson 1
1. B
2. D
3. C
4. A
5. D
6. B

Lesson 2
1. B
2. D
3. B
4. B
5. C
6. B

Lesson 3
1. B
2. D
3. B
4. A
5. C
6. A

Lesson 4
1. B
2. B
3. D
4. B
5. D
6. C

Lesson 5
1. B
2. D
3. D
4. B
5. A
6. B

Lesson 6
1. B
2. C
3. A
4. B
5. B
6. D

Lesson 7
1. B
2. D
3. C
4. A
5. C
6. C

Lesson 8
1. A
2. D
3. D
4. B
5. D
6. B

Lesson 9
1. A
2. D
3. C
4. B
5. C
6. C

Lesson 10
1. B
2. D
3. D
4. B
5. A
6. B

Lesson 11
1. B
2. C
3. C
4. B
5. C
6. C

Lesson 12
1. B
2. B
3. D
4. A
5. D
6. D